My Favorite Apocalypse

My
Favorite
Apocalypse

POEMS BY

Catie Rosemurgy

Graywolf Press

SAINT PAUL, MINNESOTA

Publication of this volume is made possible in part by a grant provided by the Minnesota State Arts Board through an appropriation by the Minnesota State Legislature, and by a grant from the National Endowment for the Arts. Significant support has also been provided by the Bush Foundation; Dayton's Project Imagine with support from Target Foundation; the McKnight Foundation; a grant made on behalf of the Stargazer Foundation; and other generous contributions from foundations, corporations, and individuals. To these organizations and individuals we offer our heartfelt thanks.

Published by Graywolf Press
2402 University Avenue, Suite 203
Saint Paul, MN 55114
All rights reserved.

www.graywolfpress.org

Published in the United States of America

"Jumping Jack Flash"
Written by Mick Jagger and Keith Richards
© 1968 ABKCO Music, Inc.
Used by permission. All rights reserved.

Excerpt from "The Gyres" reprinted with the permission of Scribner, a Division of Simon & Schuster from *The Collected Poems of W. B. Yeats*, Revised Second Edition, edited by Richard J. Finneran. Copyright 1940 by Georgie Yeats; copyright renewed © 1968 by Bertha Georgie Yeats, Michael Butler Yeats, and Anne Yeats.

ISBN: 1-55597-323-X

2   4   6   8   9   7   5   3   1
First Graywolf Printing, 2001

Library of Congress Card Number: 00-105090

Cover art: Christa Schoenbrodt, Studio Haus; Craig Brabson

Cover design: Christa Schoenbrodt

Acknowledgments

Grateful acknowledgment to the editors of the publications in which the following poems appeared, often in earlier versions:

The American Literary Review: "Grace Lies on the Sofa and Waits for Her Boyfriend to Get Home from Work"

Cream City Review: "Little Bay de Noc Softball Field," "Mostly Mick Jagger," and "Pretty"

The Distillery: "Glimmer"

The Florida Review: "Grace Lies in the Backseat While Her Boyfriend Drives the Backroads of Southwestern Florida"

Great River Review: "We Are Gathered Here Today"

Indiana Review: "Steel Blue"

Michigan Quarterly Review: "Festoon"

New Orleans Review: "Doll Up" and "What I Wanted to Say Instead of *Yes* When a Guy at the Bar Asked Me If I Grew Up near Lake Michigan"

Phoebe: "Billy Considers Leaving the World Alone," "Billy Recalls It Differently," and "Grace Lies Down to Write Her Boyfriend a Letter"

Pleiades: "The Angel and the River Water," "Jesus, the Perfect Lover," "The Mistress Notes," and "My Mom's Cobalt-Blue Glass Collection"

Ploughshares: "Blow Your House Down" and "God, as Quoted by Two Lovers"

Poetry Northwest: "Grace Lies Down in Her Tent and Talks to the Psychiatric Experts She Saw on TV," "Grace Lies Down on the Hood of Her Car," "Grace Lies on the Ice," and "When She Gets Home from the Grocery Store and Notices the Fireflies, Grace Lies Down next to the Driveway"

River Styx: "The E-String Strut (or Heaven According to the E String on Steve Earle's Acoustic Guitar)," and "Hard Put"

Sonora Review: "Twelve and Listening to the Stones"

Spoon River Poetry Review: "Fifteen Minutes after the Movie" and "The Office Party"

Verse: "The Feeling of Accomplishment I Get When He Is Pretty"

The Wisconsin Review: "Ashtray Elvis"

"Mostly Mick Jagger" also appeared in *The Best American Poetry 1997*, editor James Tate and series editor David Lehman, publisher Scribner, 1997.

"Hard Put" also appeared with "An Angel Finally Admits What She Knows to Lou Binkler of Bethany, Missouri" and "Why God Created the Cold" in *American Poetry: The Next Generation*, editors Gerald Costanzo and Jim Daniels, publisher Carnegie Mellon University Press, 2000.

I would like to thank the friends, readers, and teachers who made this book possible. Specific thanks go to Amy Benson, Rick Adams, Carrie Cooper, Angela Owens, my family (Lynn, Bob, Annie, David, Cathleen, Steve, Ian, Colin, Percy, and Jane), Mickey Newbury, Doug Fix, Jonis Agee, Diane Glancy, Alvin Greenberg, Robin Behn, Michael Martone, Sandy Huss, Elizabeth Meese, and everyone at the University of Alabama, Guili Coniglio, Beth Richards, David Slater, and William Trowbridge. I thank the West Virginia Writers' Workshop and the Anderson Center for providing wonderful places to write. I would also like to thank Jeff Shotts and all the great people at Graywolf.

Special thanks, always, to Thomas Rabbitt.

for Lynn and Robert Rosemurgy,
my mother and father

Contents

What matter though numb nightmare ride on top,
And blood and mire the sensitive body stain?
What matter? Heave no sigh, let no tear drop,
A greater, a more gracious time has gone. . . .
What matter? Out of Cavern comes a voice
And all it knows is that one word 'Rejoice.'

—W.B. Yeats, "The Gyres"

I was drowned.
I was washed up and left for dead.
I fell down
to my feet and I saw they bled.
I frowned
at the crumbs of a crust of bread.
I was crowned
with a spike right through my head.
But it's all right now,
in fact it's a gas.
It's all right now.
I'm Jumping Jack Flash.
It's a gas, gas, gas.

—The Rolling Stones, "Jumping Jack Flash"

My Favorite Apocalypse

Festoon

Every two feet, a pair of calla lilies
covers a tack pinning a cream satin ribbon
to the church wall. Every now and then

over the past twelve years, the groom has
backed me up against a wall.
My skin, my showy, scented skin,

brightened each time he wanted to kiss me.
As crisp as a stem, I leaned into him
on the front porch, in the restaurant,

on the college quad. Every two minutes,
either I think of his hands
or I think the bride does.

His covert, cocktail-party caresses
are his greatest gift. I work backwards
to his finger tracing my neckline. She works forwards.

I'm a lily. I'm a tack. Her voice feels
like a cream satin ribbon swinging across
the middle of my back. She has my blue, amused eyes.

I could have her life. I say, "With this ring."
I deliver his baby. I set out
his vitamins, and my hands are wrinkled.

But I don't know her. I know his mouth.
I could be his mouth.
I kiss her deeply. She is as bright inside

as a lily. The undiluted taste of her
holds me in place while fields and streams
come and go around us. Like him, I spread out quickly

into the dirt. From thirty feet away,
she reminds me of a mirror, of practicing
what I will say. I say, "I take thee." But taking his hand,

she is finished. She is decorated and wise.
She knows that whenever she lays down her hands
they will land on some part of him,

even in the dark,
for the rest of her life.
Husband and wife, they walk out,

the congregation pulled after them
in drowsy, well-dressed chains.
My date guides me. Each man's hand

supports the small of a woman's back.
Each woman's stare is fixed
on another man's neck. There will be miles

between the couples in minutes.
This is my last chance to lead myself
to disaster. When he hugs me good-bye,

the groom says my name in my ear.
My name. My job. My city. Lights in the skyline.
People living. Bodies briefly

captured in bright windows.
I want to tell him I love him because
I may never think of his handsome face again.

Twelve and Listening to the Stones

Yeah, you got satin shoes. Yeah, you got plastic boots.
—The Rolling Stones, "Can't You Hear Me Knocking"

If I had a best friend, I might not tell her
that once you find your insides
and can tighten them, you can bring the ground
up to your face, bring the earth you're standing on
up through your body, until you can breathe
the grass as it comes through the dirt.
I might not tell her
I have muscles no one can see.
Not only can I keep rhythm and bring it
inside me one beat at a time, I can also clench
right in front of the paperboy's face until I feel a fist
loosening its grip on the largeness
inside me. The most he can see about me,
even if he looks impossibly close,
are the barely colored wisps of hair against my forehead.
They might tremble.
I tighten while I wait for the school bus.
I've worn the snow into ice.
How quiet I can be.
I close my eyes and change the size of things.
My house disappears below me.
The dark moves inside me like hands.

Cranberry Juice

My boyfriend lists my favorite recipes. He zeros in
on exactly what he should make me for dinner.
But I'm distracted from the good life
by the random bullet I imagine burning in my side.

The bullet popped a clean hole
in the kitchen window, the saltshaker, then in me.
I stare at my boyfriend's veins until they seem
to take over his hands. I perform the signs of panic,

work to make my eyes bulge, "Finish me off."
He doesn't notice. He's a nice guy.
Whenever I feel a bit bruised
around the temple, his mouth is always there,

scooping up some smile for me to taste.
He's my front porch swing. Rock. Rock.
See. I'm not really self-destructive.
I want to keep all my teeth.

Still, I want him to call me pink and stupid.
Let him take some responsibility for the tongue
wasting in my throat. Division of labor.
I'll tell him to shut up whenever he needs me to.

I'm into fake blood lately, guzzling
cranberry juice and risking stains. After a liter
I go to the mirror and chuckle about my safe mouth
looking torn. But I can't leave him out—

today's Sunday.
When we take our drive, the country music
will be loud. I always sing louder.
He says he can stand the graves

under apple trees, the roses on freight trains
if he hears all the sugar from me.
But I'm going to ask him please,
just once, hold a gun to my head.

Make trigger noises.
Force me to sing "To live is to fly," to knock
life unconscious with a phrase. Tell me I better
mean "peach ice cream" and "I believe" when I say it.

When we get home, I'll return the favor.
I'll kiss him on the collarbone, walk him to the hall closet,
and lock him inside. The only thing he'll be responsible for
is banging on the door.

Grace Lies on the Sofa and Waits
for Her Boyfriend to Get Home from Work

The thermometer he suction-cupped
to the sliding glass door says
fifteen below zero. She has the heat
turned up so high
the hairs of her sweater have curled.
Whenever she moves, she leaves behind her
the scent of blown-out birthday candles.
Her patience is two weeks old today.

While the temperature's been fatal,
her mind's been full of possibilities: suspicious
mounds of snow, her boyfriend cracking
into a million pieces as he steps outside.
In her favorite daydream, the door's too cold
for her to press her forehead against the glass
and grieve. In her real life, the frost grows
more complicated on the window.

The frozen yard is like a shy god
who sneaks up in his white blanket and breathes
against the glass. He creates crystals so that maybe later
he can watch them touch her. He's never known
such color as her iris and her lip.
The frost wants to come inside and cling
to the edges of her throw pillows.
She's threatened with becoming

a rimed then a shattered rose,
the victim of a legion of twinkles. The tiny, spiked,
mathematically omniscient angels
will carry her off
the way a lake carries off
a sheet of ice. Her boyfriend

will have to stare at her all day
to notice that she's going.

She tries to be an anomaly, a melter,
an uncharted island of heat. She tries to maintain
an arsenal of memories — his back, her hands.
But she cooks off all the moisture in the house,
and her skin suffers. Her calves itch.
Her face pinches like an outfit she looks good in
but wears only to take off.
She's left trembling like ash.

What can she do when his skin
isn't thawing in the corner? Lounge and live only
for the wet snow drifted halfway up
the young birch trees? Live only to get an ache
under her tongue? Ache and admit she's in love
with being in a box, with being held at bay,
with burning up and imagining parts of herself
floating brightly toward the curtains?

He'll be pink as a baby's knuckle
when he comes back home. He'll say he feels
as if he's being stuck with pins. His beard will be frozen
as it would be if she found him dead.
She'll be singed and slightly smaller on the couch.
Coughing, he'll come to her.
With their hands and their faces,
they'll invent 98.6 degrees.

Billy Sees Stars

Grace's on my lap and staring at my collar.
She's scheming the best way to slither down
between my skin and the cotton without
my knowledge, my deep breathing. She likes heaven
to be a big surprise. She doesn't know,
but I take her like a low, low star
into my hands. In my mind she can turn
iridescent and small without much warning.
Once the ache for orbit leaves her, I hold her
up above my head and brag to the sun.
I say, "You're not the only one who
can make fire worthwhile." Without warning,
she's an armload of flesh. She doesn't know,
but I hold her and I brag to the sun.

The Angel and the River Water

—for Bethie

I picture Libby undressed, thirteen, floating dead in the river.
Leaves cling to her like burnt-out stars
looking for a way to get at her light.
She wants to give it to them,
but she can't move it through her skin.
The pressing only makes her bigger, softer, brighter.

Libby and I used to wear half shirts,
bluer than the veins in our tongues,
and more ruffled around our middles
than a bridal hem
held an inch above the ground.
We'd lie in the middle of her bedroom floor,
our arms, legs, and bellies blending
into the cool pine boards. While we disappeared,
we described ourselves so well,
walking in our heart-attack-colored shirts,
ignoring the windows downtown.
We must have materialized, arm-in-arm,
on the sidewalk eventually—the windows on Main Street
looked like dropped chins all the time.
Maybe we were cruel,
the way we swayed to the radio
with our eyes closed, the way we looked like angels
when nobody was there to see. At least once,
I must have looked good enough to lock up,
because I moved like her and I stopped like her
and when I peeked at her
she was done, perfected, like anything
ready to fly away.
Guys don't know what to do
around a girl who can dance.
That's what we used to say
on Friday nights in her room.

Libby could take a gravy-stained, gray-haired waitress
and turn her into the only thing in the room
worth discussing. "See her," she'd say
out of nowhere, looking up from her fries.
"Her husband can't make it work
so he uses candles on her instead."
I hated to leave Libby at night. She started to glow
when she made up her stories. After two or three,
so did I. She said I had a hot candle inside me
and I had to use my body
as a disguise. We'd lie perfectly still
next to one another. We wouldn't talk for hours.

I ride my bike at night
over the water and pretend there's no bridge.
I imagine she'll make me fall one day,
when she thinks I'm ready. But I've gotten as lonely
as I can. Every Saturday I fly back and forth
over the river. Sometimes mist joins me,
sometimes it doesn't. When I land on the riverbank, I'm magical,
but there's no one I want to tell.

My mom sat with me for a long time.
When she told me what Libby had done—
strapped on exercise weights and refused
to float—I knew Libby wanted her body to stay
on the river bottom where it could disappear but still
catch someone's eye.
My mom pulled me against her as if I were dangerous,
as if I were her soul walking away.
She hoped I would pass through
her rib cage for a second.
When she told me what some guy had done,
what Libby bragged to her mother he had done and done,
my mom fidgeted. She said the world

is full of users. She didn't say where
he touched Libby or for how long
or if Libby went limp in his hands.

Libby used to laugh at anything—
her bedroom walls, her own face,
the way I always locked the door,
the way she always caught me looking at her
when I was supposed to be dancing.
I guess he, whoever he is, couldn't concentrate either.
She seemed to suck up all the light in the room,
and she never seemed to want it. Poor monster,
he used her to prove he could keep
something warm next to him.
He used her to feel good about himself.
We've got that in common.

Iceblink

I walk to my bay window to test myself.
I use only a sloped world, fresh snow,
and a house that blocks out the moon.
I see if I can make blue light.

I pass the test. The glow in my bones
is out tonight. I expose the white backyard
for what it is—a long, close-up look at me,
minus the shivers, minus the muscle and the skin.

Icicles, twigs, and cattail stalks
glint back at me, their breakable leader.
The moon is my marrow, I shall not want.
Not lips or breasts. Not one curve.

I shine strong enough to prove
no lovers exist. No tender movements.
No footprints. I could live alone forever
watching over a field of snow.

God, as Quoted by Two Adulterers

Let no air ever come between you. No clean sheet. No lamplight.
No dust. Let the hotel curtain be your guide, the absolute fabric,
the craving to get lost like a strong thread. Go blank against

one another. Turn blue. That's day and night. Stop needing
your own blood so. Dry up and get in one another's eyes.
You'll be blind soon, so feel more. Your very fingerprints

are at stake. Let the head lie down with the white bed,
let the belly lie with the whole empty day. Let the shoulder cave in
against the mouth, the mouth against the eyelash. Peace is not stillness.

The hip joint, the smile—for heaven's sake—daisies, river stones,
beer bottles, gravel, church bells. Everything is loose. The world is
a rope and a plank. A swing. Far outside your borrowed window,

whole species of grass collapse for the wind. Don't think you are
any different. Kiss hard. Burrow if you have any sense. Shudder
while you still can. Let freckles lie with tears. Deceive, at least, yourselves.

Say "There's always next time." Press like pages. Fade like violets.
Break like leaves when one of you walks away. Pour like honey
over one another when both of you are full. Stick. Stick. Stick.

Grace Lies Frozen in the Front Yard

She's stunned, made of colors,
and afraid to move anything
but her eyes. She has landed in the snow
like a tropical bird. She was going somewhere,
a camellia bush beside a lagoon,
a branch so new
she would seem to hover
in the air. But someone threw a switch. The humidity
shrank into ice, and she dropped,

frozen, mid-flight. Exactly
the way she'd planned it: her coat bright
and broken, her face a serious mistake
in a field of snow, his name
caught inside the cube forming
in her throat. Better her than him.
When the branches stopped
their kind, slow scratching
of the sky, she could tell

that somebody, sooner or later,
was going to freeze. She'd lose him
either to someone else's latest kiss
or to his own stillness. Lying next to him
would lead to waking up, and waking up would lead
to finding a lump in the bed.
Either dead or disinterested.
She hasn't decided yet if it's good or bad
that nothing lasts forever.

Billy Calls Grace *Darling*

I'd take a baby rabbit in my arms
and dribble milk into its toothy mouth
from an eyedropper all night if I thought
I could get rid of the kindness in my hands.
I'd think of myself as a soft mother bird
who had to give up her speed, her camouflage,
and her hungry babies if I thought
the tragedy would make her want to own me.
She'll come home late and fall down without me.
She'll slide like an icicle next to me in bed.
I'll want to turn over and make sure
she's made of skin and rhythm, not just cold air.
But she'll half kiss my shoulder if she believes
I'm asleep, so I won't ever touch her.

The Feeling of Accomplishment I Get When He Is Pretty

He's the one who breathed the past
down my arm, the one who held
his skin and bone together
so handsomely. He's the one
I had to get rid of.
In the beginning, I sat
on his lap and bit his lip.

My mouth watered in his mouth.
When he kicked open my legs,
I dedicated my hands
to making more of him,
to rubbing away the hard,
sweaty bottle that held him in.
He could have gotten loose

in my living room. He could have made
my living-room curtains shiver
over me and my breasts.
My shivers, at least, slid around
the lips of cups and rocked recliners.
I listed places he was salty,
counted the seconds I soaked

in each of them. He was all
teeth and Guinness, then all neck
and soap. Rearranged,
he kept coming back to me
through my pores.
Because he was a star,
I was automatically

nebulous. But his body
kept ending, cowardly,
in tiny bones. I could have
shined him hard,
piece by piece,
but I wore straight
through him instead.

On the other side of him, the night sky
waited for my fingertips
to grow warm and bright.
I took part in heaven.
Soon his empty palms
died out on my sheets.
I was proud to be alone.

Little Bay de Noc Softball Field

—for Annie

Fourth inning. The girls have salt and dust
crumbling off their upper lips. Little rocks
of sweat and pieces of the diamond.
Crouched and ponytailed to take
a solid hit in the teeth,
they hop from foot to foot
like crows because they want it:
the specks of dirt that get in their eyes, the polyester uniforms
that pick at their scraped thighs, the good chance
of a bat to the head. "Come on, junior,"
the girls tease the ball just before
the bat touches it. "I'm ready
to leave town whenever you are."

Fifth inning. The smell of grass
gets up everybody's nose.
Three boyfriends are here
to watch each player—one past, one present,
one future. The town is this small.
With their tank tops thrown over their shoulders,
the boyfriends balance on ten-speeds
against the fence. Occasionally one falls
and says, "Whew," then looks impressed
up at the sun. The coach yells
at the infield to turn their hats forward.
Dads lifting toddlers out of puddles remember
the first time they had to duck, drop, hide
because their daughter connected with a pitch.
Restraightening their spines
never felt as good. The next batter up clacks bats
with the batter on deck. In the bleachers,
moms laugh loud and ragged. Twenty years ago
they played up on bunts
and smoked Camels. They happily shove each other

for being outrageous about golf scores
and the chemicals in the fish they ate Friday night.
They're thinking—Stacy, Allison, Kimmy,
for Christ's sake, get your gloves down.
Annie, keep your elbow up.
Your muscles stretch so easily right now.

The Mistress Notes

Ahem. Let me swear on your skin
as I speak. Let me lie on you like a left hand
on the Bible. Let me kneel

while you open me like the good book.
I know, I know, when you believe you are being saved,
you can't help but smile.

There is nothing in this world but Spring, though, darling,
nothing but Genesis and more muddy Genesis,
doggy-style and more barky doggy-style.

Let me explain the history of civilization:
eyes roll back into heads, boards are nailed up,
eyes roll more privately and dramatically back into heads.

There is nothing but petals and women doing
impersonations of muddy petals. You know I love
the way I stick against your pelvic bone,

the river of your touch rising.
I am the branch, the bloom, and the berry. I dangle
over your flooding

with a thousand other women,
but you wash me away.
How am I to know if I am poisonous or sweet?

There is nothing in this world to build but a nest, darling.
I have seen proud green shoots, and who knows
what they would grow to be. I have seen buds so tight

they made my eyelashes flutter, and who knows
what they have inspired me to be. I have hoped
your sagging gray house would buckle,

snap under the weight of camellias
or sin or fresh paint, and who knows, who knows
how publicly I would take you

if you were homeless and lying prone,
pinned down by my friends, guilt and shame.
There is nothing but Spring and perhaps

the resting up for Spring.
I am an animal on top of you,
underneath you, beside you, far away from you.

I am nothing if not Spring.
And yet nothing about me is ever
truly new. I have wanted to slip

on the wet grass, longed to fall, darling, and know
the ecstasy of bending
in an impossible new way right before

the bone snaps.
Haven't you, darling? Haven't you?
Look at you, roughly parting

my pliable legs, forgetting
your brittle past.
Of course you have.

What I Wanted to Say Instead of *Yes*
When a Guy at a Bar Asked Me
If I Grew Up near Lake Michigan

May I draw a line across the middle
of your face? I'm used to half the world
being blue and lapping at my feet.

The reassuring calm of your forehead
almost perfectly replaces the lake
and may leave me with nothing to do but sleep.

Only the sound of waves is missing
from your skin. How peaceful. How empty.
Let your busy lips be all that's left

of the city. Rome, New York, Troy,
the local beach. Your mouth is big enough
to explain the history of decline.

Two months have gone by since I last got rid
of the land and the sails and went under,
since I last lifted my leg from the water

and created composition, curve, and skin.
And you can tell. There are no drops running
down my face. There's nothing glistening to catch

with the tip of your finger. I'm not new.
No wonder I can't get you to shut up.

Grace Lies in Her Tent and Talks
to the Psychiatric Experts She Saw on TV

The day before I moved out of the house
I share with my boyfriend and into this tight
new shape in our backyard,
I walked into a bookstore.
Every page said the same thing:
true crime was self-help.
Back home I turned on the TV
to the usual panels of open-mouthed women.
You guys sat next to them, your heads
stuck out past your knees,
as if explaining requires contortions.

I admit I began to think of the bedroom as a box
and of the house as a big blue package.
I began to feel like a lousy present,
folded in sheets like a surprise
in tissue paper—"Look,"
you could say,
"a little ceramic bitch."
Can you see her itsy-bitsy scowl right there?

I was almost a famous woman once.
For a year and a half.
I was the woman who has a face and two hands.
I lived in a house.
I saw myself shrunk
in the flashes of all our faucets and wore weak light
spilled through a cracked door for makeup.
Of course my hands were swollen;
I had to keep my pulse somewhere.
The thumping would have been too ugly in my face.

Yes, I do remember how I became threatening.
I was lying in bed.
I was trying to forget that my swollen hands
could feel each muscle in my boyfriend's neck
when he swallowed. That's when I knew
I could be famous, the woman with her hands
around her lover's throat
for no particular reason.

The strangest, smallest things
make me wonder what he did to deserve it. Chickadees
with their beaks clamped
to the tips of each other's wings.
A few pine needles
sticking like hairs out of the snow.
Not that I actually killed him or even leaned

on his Adam's apple to push myself out of bed.
But it's a crime against something
to want to hurt him.
I think of the need for control
epitomized by Dan Rather's hair, the encouraging pluck
of Connie Chung's eyebrow. All January
the two of them tried to console me.
I confessed that what he did and deserves
aren't the right questions.
I hate the publicity,
always hearing about the woman just like me.

You lean over your feet in an attempt
to come out of the TV.
As experts you say, "Well, well."
Should I take away the line
that makes the side of the house?

Should I turn the line up at the ends and make a sled,
our whole life pulled by dogs?
That would make things move.

In our backyard, I kiss the back of my hand.
My knuckles are the features of his face.

Billy Recalls It Differently

The rattle of my tin shed where I kept
my crocus bulbs was like the rattle
of my teeth as I slid into bed. Packed blooms.
Sweet fists. I liked to be able to look at
the delicate things I would never say.
My house rose up through pine needles and dust.
My house reared up in its white paint and cobwebs.
I shivered as I slipped from its belly
into the snow at quarter to seven
every morning. I blinked to strut my stuff.
Every morning there was a second
of darkness. Every morning it calmed
me down. Every morning cold wind for blood.
Every morning was not like this one.
A girl-shaped leaf had fallen onto my bed.

To My Lover on Returning to His Wife and Then Finding Another Lover

—after Anne Sexton's
"To My Lover on Returning to His Wife"

Once upon a time, there was a concept
dressed in impenetrable silk tulle,
and her name was called Fidelity.
I killed her. The sun was in my eyes,
and it was a hunting accident.
She wore a surprised look and a jaunty
little crown of busted arrows.
What truly bothered me, though,
was that I couldn't attend
her funeral, where there were
such real tears and deserved Kleenex.
Where I could stand in sensible shoes
and say, "So THIS is why God invented
morals!" Instead, I kept my mouth shut
at home. I did a study that I call
"A Study in the Different Types
of Cruelty." First on the list
was anything invasive one could do
to birds and next was you.
I was a very poetic scientist,
a real numskull, and I lost
all my funding. I used it up
buying myself dresses to take off.

My Mom's Cobalt-Blue Glass Collection

I was ten, eleven, twelve, thirteen,
bored and sprawled in a kitchen chair.
My blood would soon stop moving
if I didn't fall in love or otherwise
risk my life. Meanwhile, all over the room,
the color blue had it easy. The color blue
had gone all the way, in public, and glowed
from holding in its sighs.
It had fallen asleep in a snowbank
while recalling its lover's eyes.
The color blue was numb
but still mumbling secrets.
It was the color of a sun that has too much
on its mind and accidentally rises
underneath a frozen lake. I was fourteen,
fifteen, sixteen, seventeen,
and the house was dead quiet.
My mom loved me. My dad loved me.
The color blue was still dreaming.
No one had dared me to do anything,
not to wait for him under a snowbank
or meet him at the bottom of a lake.
I wondered why I was willing.
Everywhere, the final color of Juliet's lips.
The color of a girl turning into light.

~

My mom collected the glass
for more cheerful reasons, I think.
She perched among her dark and shining
bowls as if they were eggs,
as if they were cracking and miraculously
she were growing fat again.
She smiled, she spoke, she fed me.

She never once explained
her glowing kitchen window except to say,
"Maybe I should start a green window in the living room."
My dad said, "Moderation in all things,
especially moderation" and bought her
a ten-piece set of blue-glass jars at Christmas
to replace her white ones, bought her
a stout blue husband and wife
to use as saltshakers. I assumed he meant
"OK, lady, drown us," even though
all he ever wanted was room
to set the mail on the counter. We couldn't move
without rattling and shining. Lit up, my little sister said,
"I couldn't live like this." Glowing, I said, "Totally."
My parents had to try not to smile
when they looked at one another. I didn't know why.
Maybe the heaven they kept
behind their faces was expanding
and about to escape. Maybe the fission
tickled their wet mouths. Maybe it was a joke,
a tease, a trick, the fact
that she would be upstairs, surrounded
by silent pieces of every beautiful night ever
and he would be downstairs, which he kept
bare of everything except the sound
coming from his stereo. He said, "Call me for dinner.
I'll be downstairs." In the end,
they couldn't help it. They smiled
as they moved into separate rooms. I had no idea
what was so funny, what was so blue.

Once I had turned into light,
things came easily to me,

things like light and more light,
fire beneath the skin, eyes burned
into sheets at night, the way a certain boy
might kiss me. When it's lit up, the color blue
is a museum of what could have been.
Sky, him. Sea, me. We could have been
seventy-five percent of the earth
and then some. Behind my parents' house,
the beach and I did more than age several years.
When I scattered myself over a wave,
I looked like something an honest person
would want to steal. I looked as if God
had been caught with a mouthful
of diamonds and had to spit them out.
When I found out my mom was sick,
this is what I thought: strands of my hair
will rise and glisten if I walk down the street.
Someone might see me catching the light
if I ever decide to leave here.

⁀

I came home at 1 A.M. and my parents
were drinking in the kitchen. "Wine?" I asked my sister.
"Smoking inside?" She nodded as if she'd seen
the world end several times. My dad had carried
his cassette player upstairs again
to play my mom another tape he'd made for her.
The only thing I still do
like I used to do
is carry this torch for you. The song had echoed up
the basement stairs all my life.
He couldn't have kept it down there if he'd tried.
My parents sat in front of the song on sagging kitchen chairs
as if passion were no big deal. They didn't care

what the singer revealed about their dancing and crying.
Humming, they looked at me, at each other,
and at the gleam packed into the room.

⁓

Their tears and kisses are loose everywhere.
I'm a perfect example.
And for a kiss, I've lasted a long time.
I don't see myself ever ending,
given all the chilly neon
I've soaked up, all the floodlight,
the white sheet, and the moonlit trillium.
Given all the waiting I've done
in front of radiant dinner plates.
In front of late-night TV and good teeth.
Underneath the simple constellations
of two sticky palms
that were often my own.
I'd be blinding if it weren't for sleep
and its stubborn, dark air.
A body, any body, is a welcome,
deep-blue pool to me. I am a fire to myself,
and I like to spend my days drowning.
What a mess of elements it takes
to be alone, the glare off my skin
getting brighter, a man, any man,
trying to cover me up, trying to shade me,
trying to turn me blue and glassy. I know my mom is dying,
dying now or dying later, and still the slow
dying in between. When I see her look of worry
on my face, I know that there is a sweetness in me
and that I am going to have to learn to live with it.

⁓

The sky is the color my mom keeps
between the Tylenol and the dirty dishes,
and it's impossible that I love no one in particular,
that I've missed out on watching him die.
My parents are spinning
on a dance floor. I can feel them.
They're spinning at the bottom of a lake.
When they look at each other,
the weight of the cold, blue water
asks them politely to close their eyes. And it seems fitting.
Something tangible should also be this big.
I'm going to kiss the next tangible man I see,
even though when I'm done I'll feel only
the slide of his teeth
in my mouth and my own shame.
When my mom got sicker, slowly, cell by cell,
my dad could barely acknowledge it.
He was quiet when he tried to clean
her kitchen counters. She wept over how slow
and predictable she must look to him when she tried to move.
They gathered it to them, made a house out of it,
the blue color of the spaces between their bodies.
A man who lives across the street
stands and watches what his rosebushes do
when it gets dark. I'll ask him to hold me.
I'll gesture at the sky,
then to myself. I'll gesture at myself
and then to the sky. I'll say, excuse me,
but don't you need,
don't you need to know this sorrow?

Lying in Her Sleeping Bag,
Grace Makes Her Tent Her Home

1

The shadows, snow, and orange canvas combine
to make the color of my sister Sarah's nipples.
When we were kids, I used to pretend to want
her nipples in my mouth when I pretended
to be her husband pretending to rape her
or to rape the smell of the lake on her.
The rest of her body was the color of wet sand.
I made her into a stranger so easily
that she did the same for me.

2

He wouldn't let me turn off the light
on my last night inside, warm and blue-eyed
in our bed. He wanted me to see him shake.
I told him you can cry, but I wish you wouldn't.
I told him I would sneak back one night,
under the door and up his leg

like a cold wind. That's what I'm doing out near the bases of trees:
gathering enough speed. I told him he could drift
through the loose storm window
like a honeyed smell hot from the oven and get caught
in my hair. He said he would stay with me always.
I said he could sometimes surprise me.
He said I should talk to someone.
I said he could do that for me.
I told him to pretend I wasn't gone.
He was just holding me in his mouth

for safekeeping. He said can you see
how I'm shaking? I said if you tell my sister I'm sleeping
closer to the edge of a frozen pond than I am to you,

I'll disappear for good. All I'll be to you
is a flash of blond hair between
the birch trees, and a flash is the one thing
no one ever forgets. Which was the wrong thing to say.

Because now when I'm especially cold
and feel like a footprint in the snow,
and just want to be a track left by a sled,
I keep breathing. I keep having hands
and everything else.
Because he never forgets me.
He never forgets a single part of me.

3

"Come home, Grace."
They're calling me—sisters, boyfriends.
Boys are sweeter than I thought
when I used to wait for my turn to be one.
Sisters are farther away. Too far away to be frightened
that I may only trail into the woods
until I fill with snow. I've gone too far this time with my pretending.
Everything is in its place.

If Billy Were Invisible

I have one daydream I feel good about.
Unseen, I gather anything alive
she ever lost, anything secret
she'd still want held together, even by tape,
anything that made her understand
the need for lockets, and I lay it all out
in the room she is about to walk into.
I don't watch her cry. I slip through the wall
before I become real again, which is the part
I'm proud of. The part where I don't want
to take credit for helping her crumble
into those loose pieces she loves so much.
But I'm kidding myself. The woman I love is finally
weeping and, still, the dream is only about me.

Lake Superior Confesses to the Shore
of Keeweenaw Bay

No one can make me give up my rowboats. Those tiny kisses
break into blue, red, and yellow flowers
when I hold them close. The balsam fir

and the northern white pine try to be straight
and judgmental. They crowd around and whisper.
Now and then one of them turns the color of rust.

They think they are all the needles
ever lost in haystacks. So serious, serious
about dirt and air, about being solid in between.

I'm a very slow-filling bowl, a massive shudder
over each grain of sand.
I'm wave after wave of proof

that you can grow accustomed to futile desires
as long as you occasionally get to hear
the sound of splitting wood.

I crash because I need
whatever grit the rocks can spare. I only bother
with seven-foot waves because I hope

to drag a common loon, a common goldeneye,
a blue-winged teal, any solid piece of sky,
down inside me to mark the place

where my heart would be. The couple on the beach
watches me. My utter lack of hands
must break their hearts. They must feel it.

Meanwhile, I'm lying. Shipwrecks
I've hired in secret
caress a hundred feet of me at a time.

An ore boat has been touching me
in the same place for eighteen years. Of course I reach out,
but not because I've hated myself

ever since I misplaced the sun. Not because I want
to steal a molecule of daylight, tuck the truly
rare pearl inside me, feel it

gradually sink through me,
until it discovers where I end.
I wouldn't mind systematically tearing the earth apart,

searching through a blue sky for the crucial atom,
and then watching a summer day collapse.
But I take and take what I can get.

Steel Blue

My dad named me Steel Blue,
after his song and his guitar.
I didn't have a mother to fight him, to say, "No,
she's Lizabeth Olivia, a beautiful girl,
not a metal string, not the sad way you bend it."
And a mother would have won
because girls belong to mothers,
to their mothers they are unconditional and beautiful.
Most girls are never allowed anything to do
with the rolling-away beauty of being wanted,
the steel-blue want
that starts with a father
someplace cold and hard and slides.
Most girls just get to be the kind of beautiful
that mothers need them to be
after being turned gut-side out by delivering a girl.

I didn't have a mother, thank god.
At the most she was a sound I heard once
through a door: car keys or the folding of a map.
Like a tumbleweed, I came from what you can't see,
the hollow of a desert-sized guitar.
From behind a huge dry time of day,
maybe from a drought crack cutting
an absence of lightning across the earth.
I still come, rolling past the shape of another man.
A tangle of loneliness, I remind him
of a sound building inside him,
against his thighs, against his stomach
until it rings
in the center of his palms.
He learns to play so he can hear
how much he wants me, which is by far
my favorite song.

I recognize it
because it sounds helpless
like a long story starting—
a car driving away at night,
someone in a house staring at the dark
that comes in like a lover
through a half-open door,
someone small standing in a yard
until she is her own idea of a leaf or a hole.
All in notes.
In the slide, the hold, the rhythm of the first few notes.

Men are verses.
They fit or they don't.
When I hear music,
I see myself—a tumbleweed, a panic of sticks.
A constant rolling away.
Lizabeth Olivia would probably love
these men who just want a few prints from Paris,
a yellow lab, and wood floors. Lizabeth Olivia
could probably see more in them, could probably be beautiful
in the plain kitchen light her mother always sat in.
Not me. I roll the earth.
I listen for the end.

Jesus, the Perfect Lover

2000 years and he's still rising.
I know, I know, girls. If Hell didn't exist before,
it does now. Just for my mouth. But if I explained

how his skin feels, how timeless and damp,
how raw and in need of bandaging
from my constant, constantly

forgiven touch,
you'd toss your hair one last time
and put on your suit of flames too.

How often have we all said, "If only
I never had to leave the house again, if only
my wishes were fishes and my supernatural boyfriend

could make thousands more of them, if only no one else
ever existed at all." My Jesus spreads himself out
permanently and looks a lot like me:

a bit disappointed but not too surprised. Still, he's glad
that he can at least distract me from whatever
crude nails my palms have room for.

But look how he hangs so quietly—there's definitely
an ingredient missing. Someone very large
didn't think it through and forgot

to add absolute strength.
So he's my undressed apology,
my portable laboratory

where "Dear Lord, no" and "My God, yes"
were simultaneously invented.
I can tell by the amused look in his eye

that, straddling and blond
and incomplete, I am not responsible
for what I do. Mostly, though, the way

we squirm together
is like sleep, only brighter.
After I press against him

for an hour or two, he can see right through me.
He knows the glint of my ribs,
the steam escaping my heart.

Any fool can see
how he looks down at me,
wanting to hold me, extinguish me, wishing

he would've thought of this before,
of everything he could have done for me
with his arms. That's what makes him perfect,

he always admits
to my burning image
when he's wrong.

Grace Lies Down to Write Her Boyfriend a Letter

Dear Billy. Dear Man in the Window Watching Me.
Dear Hand of the Clock. Dear Straight Spine
always striking midnight. Dear Unshot Arrow. Dear
oh Dear, I miss you. Love, Grace.
It's a thin line between happy and sad,
and you are that line. Dear Line.
Dear Deadline. Dear Calendar. Dear Friendly Reminder.

Cancel my appointments. I stepped out for a minute.
You must feel some sense of relief. Dear Diagram
of How a Raindrop Falls,
I am writing to you from the bottom
of a brand-new ocean. Jealous?
The whole thing is frozen solid, Dear Ice Fisher,
and I'm caught in the ice like a piece of colored thread,

not noticeable, unless you fall against the lake
in exactly the right place.
So don't look for me so hard. Don't blame yourself.
Don't wish your fists were shaped like picks.
I remember the length of you, Dear Mile of Sand,
Dear Unopened Beach Umbrella.
So don't stand in the window and fall apart now.

And don't believe a word of this either,
this I'm-like-and-you're-like-
everything-in-the-world-besides-ourselves.
I'm just trying to make us both feel better,
since you're stuck in the house, Dear Candy Thermometer,
and I'm less and less like anything.
Dear Confidence. Dear Fan Club President. Dear Audience.

I'm no longer like the busy stripper.
No longer like the hundreds of men

who dream of eating maraschino cherries
out of the cups of her ears.
I'm no longer like the maraschino cherries,
Dear Amaretto Sour. I'm like a girl lying in a tent
with all of your names in her mouth.

Billy Considers Leaving the World Alone

If she would stop trying to hold the snow
inside her, if I'd quit trying to slip
the buzz in the bushes inside my chest,
if she would stop believing she drifted
down for weeks until she was three feet deep,
if I'd stop needing fifty wings to whir
and fifty eyes to be able to see
her at all, if we could be fair to the bee
and to the blizzard, if we could leave one
to its yellow and one to its frostbite
and not steal the little death for ourselves,
then soon enough, there would be nothing much
left of us, nothing left to keep apart.
But what a tedious paradise.

The Office Party

My friends don't look at me. They steal peeks.
They're worried the office air isn't enough
to hold me in. They dread the teeth and the pearls,
the *and then he, and then he,* the flecks of my heart
that seem destined for the wallpaper. I remember when
I was young and made up of camera flashes,
when the dismembered light of fireworks hinted
at what I could do. I was young and everywhere—
in the color silver, in the grind of metal on metal.
I was just plain young. Just plain packed down
into the cannon and successfully detonated.
Driven deep into walls and shins, I shifted
just one of my many points and watched everyone, like a chorus line,
wince, limp, and break out into a shiny sweat
below the hairline. That was only two days ago.
That was when I believed he was always a second away
from wanting to kiss me. I was scattered no doubt,
but I was scattered like the will to fuck,
like sixteen-year-olds in tight trousers.
I strutted across the office as if he loved me,
as if his fingers and my hipbones were flint
and all my friends' faces were fire.
Now my friends peek at me as I load the Xerox machine.
They wonder what I'm making so many copies of.
I used to lean against the water fountain.
I used to brag about my lunch break: if he and I
would only stumble into the broom closet, we could invent
the three-car family out of straw,
detergent, and wire. I'm no priestess, but I made a life for myself
out of things that shine, out of paper clips
and earrings. Out of the kisses I would invent
for his face. It never occurred to me
that he might not want them. Like a dumb sun
I got too close. I went *bang* and frightened off
my only earth. Now I just want

my last night and my five minutes ago back before
anyone finds them. I want my life in photographs back,
each red eye, and all the letters where I've written
the word "mine." I want my "maybe" back
in the base of my brain where it belongs. I want
my vaguely warm scraps of steel back,
back from under the desks and behind
the potted rubber trees. I want my *thud* back
in one bag. I want to lug it home and hold it
on my lap until I'm ready
to reassemble this bomb and figure out
how to make it deadly.

Creature

My glassy swamp, my deep, muddy frog,
he sits and gets stoned on the living-room floor.
I love him the most when he floats up

from the bottom, when he spooks the surface
of my day like a chewed up, telltale hat.
I'm doing the dishes as if a trail of clean plates

could lead me out. Are you dead, baby? Are you being
digested, my soggy lover? I take him
like a bad vacation, with my eyes narrow

and my mind bent on stepping carefully
until I can straighten my back and have
a crisp, dry cigarette. He's my mosquito bite,

and my repellent. He sits
on the floor and swings his eyes at me
like searchlights that burnt out months ago.

This swamp is too big and moist for me
to bother retracing our steps. We're so lost
even the decay can't find us. I'm so alive

nothing else can grow.
It's so dark I can't begin to imagine
how he was born. I knew evolution

never happened. We're so in love
I don't know who he is. I knew I could have
animate mud if I fucked a prince. But don't think

for a minute that I'm complaining.
I'm up to my itching ankles
in him, and he's alive.

Why God Invented the Cold

To give the people a break
from repositioning their lawn chairs.
To give us a glimpse
of life without bugs. Without weeping welts,
the odd fever, and yellow smears on our shoes.

To confuse the boys.
To force them to ask, "Why do teenage girls
smoke outside in January until
their nipples get stiff? Why do they
stand around with their coats undone and life

smacked onto their cheeks?
Am I that promising?"
To caution the men
that the boys will turn into
against following their semi-aroused girlfriends

into May lake water. Seasonal Affective Disorder.
To break up lonely highways
into manageable chunks. To make it clear
just how stupid it is to climb
the highest mountain. To encourage sweet futilities

like cuddling and mittens. The powerful
sleep lobby. To give drunks a softer, deeper
alternative to liver failure. Blue lips
and frosted eyelashes. Ski pants,
for Christ's sake. Dark roads, tight sweaters,

no boots, and stalled cars. Wanna ride,
need a lift? Country love or homespun
complex legal issues. His word pressed
firmly against her word. Zero degrees
and fourteen snowmobilers missing.

Natural selection. Two feet of fodder
for made-for-TV movies and more expected.
No fiber, calories, vitamins, hallucinogenic
properties, or nicotine without the tar. Just pain
in your membranes, unexpected falls,

sprained ankles, and hyperextended
thumbs. To see if you can
catch yourself. To put you down. You thought
you were mean and hard to figure out until
you found out about windchill.

To give us a way to understand
people who won't give us sex,
meter maids, Siamese cats, what it's like to kiss
your best friend's lover. To distinguish the sweat of euphoria
from the sweat of shock. To up the ante.

Because he could. Because he's lonely and it leaked
out of him. Because he wants attention
and a fluffy blanket that's big enough to cover his toes
and reach his chin. To create melting. To give us
another hint that the body is dead.

To add ice. To let him come as close as he can
to holding some of the glittering water he made.
To let us skate where we couldn't two weeks ago.
To let us glide on top of darkness.
To show us what it means to break through.

Grace Lies on the Ice

People who have lived five months inside winter
don't think it's crazy
to lie on the ice. We all walk through our yards
to the lake. When I wake up,
I check on the bay
out my bedroom, my living-room, and my kitchen windows.
I make sure there are tiny marks, like commas
on a clean sheet of paper,
that chip away at the white.
I don't need proof the marks are human beings.

In the grocery store,
people often seem surprised
by the variety of cans
and ways of printing the letter *A*.
I know they've spent the morning lying flat,
staring up, melting drops.
We all press ourselves against the ice
until our skins hug us
and we're as tight and as rare
as fresh fruit.

There are barely two months
when the water is the right temperature
to surround you and slip into you.
There's not much time
to get the speed of sailboats
and the way to Chicago inside you.
There are barely two months
when your human size is a question.
Ice is a slap across
what you realize is your tiny, red face.

No one leaves here, but we collect ways out.
Freezing temperatures make

a constant, trickling escape difficult.
Instead I shoot across the bay when the ice cracks,
I'm lifted off the ground by the sound
of a dog barking. When I come back down,
fish ache under my belly.
If I could make the earth a bit top-heavy,
I would slide off and end up
someplace else. We all know it.

Billy Talks of Daybreak

Once again, Grace grabs me with her rough legs
and gives me a definite shape. Her face
rises and sets above me a hundred times
before I open my eyes to watch her.
Infinity comes easily to her.
Kisses, blond hairs, blue veins, red eyes, and rain.
You name it. She's got it. Just in case,
the air coming through her curtains brings smells
of hoof, lace, and dog growl. Just in case,
I'm hard because of Grace, I'm strong because
I lift Grace, I'm alone because Grace is.
I really could go on and on. I'm funny
because Grace laughs. I'm awake because
she'll cry when we're done and need me to hold her.

The E-String Strut (or Heaven According to the E String on Steve Earle's Acoustic Guitar)

He can't sing a love song without me,
and he needs to sing so many. First he won over
the little pistol and the blank Texas sky,
then the bourbon, the Devil, and wives one and two,
then the heroin, himself, and wives three, four, and five,
then the cocaine and his Tennessee jail cell.
As he sings, his brand-new teeth wired into his head,
"I know I been bad, baby,
but I never, ever, meant to be bad to you,"

I stretch across him like a horizon,
a new day. The dark sound hole aches
to be the sun below me.
We're quite a team. He's North America's
allotment of hopeless desire,
and I'm the sound people wish they made
when they cry. Every time I ring out,
a juvenile delinquent is born. He stands defeated
only in front of a microphone.

He is rough with me sometimes
and hits me too hard. I don't cry,
pack, phone, hide, or bruise.
I break. Silver and sharp, I shoot
at his eye. He tries to sugarcoat it—
the end of my life. His drawl is shameless.
He says he uses "waaaay too much thuuumb."
The girls in the front row wish
they could be snapped in half. Three minutes later

I'm born again. He's hired a guy specifically
to touch me, to bring me back from the dead.
I'm the straight and narrow,

he's the end of the line. I'm an arrow
singing toward heaven, he's the tunnel
that swallows the train. Until he forgets how tender I am.
Until I have to ruin the opening line of the big song
to remind him. "Hey pretty baby,
are you ready for me? It's your good . . ."

He goes right through me
with his pink guitar pick.
The ounces of teeth, sweat, and tendon
start to add up. The ounces of tint
in his sunglasses and ink
in his tattoos come down on me hard.
He grabs another guitar, adjusts the strap,
makes sure I'm there—I'm everywhere—
and rounds his shoulders.

The crowd watches him come back to me,
the helpless one, the brainless one,
the one with the note inside her.

Ashtray Elvis

Look good in plastic. Smack onto cold porcelain
and the front page every other day. Drop dead naked
with dignity. I can still feel your bathroom tile getting warm
under your last suggestive pose
while I check out my groceries.
How much I miss you and bacon

as I wait to bring home my six-pack and fat-free cheese.
Live forever next to dish soap. Skinny and stiff on calendars,
sweaty on saltshakers, greasy on key chains, round on coffee cups.
As I wash my hands and look around the kitchen,
I can watch you gain weight and ridiculous amounts
of rhinestones. But still whisper

how many of my days you can outlive
with a shimmy of your left leg. Still confess
that when your sedated arm is held up by a chair
you can cup all my fantasies in one hand. Still admit
that when you sit by yourself in an unlit room
you can smear America across your face

even when you only mean to rub your eye. You are here
to take the pain I have alone at red lights
and give it whole highways of lonely luxury.
But come on, no staggering across my TV
like anybody's recently divorced uncle,
wasting my time with the shake in your voice.

OK, let the family laugh at you.
But after the commercial, come back with narrow hips,
sure as black leather. Make all of us
in the living room want to know
the lift of your lip
on some part of our skin.

Hard Put

Spite made the architects put the front desk
next to the hotel's only exit. The Devil
and the combined weight of me and, good Lord,
a sailor put these creases in my clothes.
There's no telling who or what put the voice
of Mary and the designs of Jezebel
in my drink last night. I watch the bedspread,
make sure he doesn't move, put on my jeans,
but I don't zip them, don't risk waking him
with that spiteful roar until I'm halfway
down the hall. I push open the front door. I put myself
in the middle of a clash between the hoods of cars
and sunlight. While I stand blinking, I pray for his hands,
for his calluses, for no one to speak to me.
Of course the hill puts me high enough to glimpse
the harbor. Other people invade, smuggle, yacht,
and brood over landscapes. The world runs on bad habits.
I continue to sneak, past two, three houses at a time.
I didn't put out last night. I put up with every song
the band played. I put my finger on a line or two
about crossing the water and extrapolated.
I pat my pockets and wish
I was the kind of person who always puts
her keys in the same place. I almost don't notice
that an angel put a geranium in her window
between her lace curtain and the glass,
a young mother put a gold barrette
in her daughter's dark hair. I can't put all
the acts of kindness on this street into words.

1, 2, 3 … I'm Perfect Starting Now

1

I got a skinny girl's boyfriend to look at me
like maybe women near death were overrated.
He'd been deluding himself by holding her
up to naked lightbulbs and counting her
red blood cells. She was his new ant farm,
his blue ribbon at the science fair. She was his
hundred-and-five-pound way of understanding
that there is more to life than truck exhaust.
When his eyelids took him away from her,
she pressed against him like proof
of what else he could be. He hung on
like roots that never before had a tree and said yes,
he definitely loved her now. She was his
manifesto, his theater of the under control.
Or so I tell myself. I looked like a vacation to him.
From the inevitability of bones and saying no. From waking up
and the other burdens of having standards.
Or so I tell myself. All he did was meet my eye and smile.

2

I got my ex-boyfriend to talk to me the other day
as if I were a human being capable of great breathing.
At first, I exhaled proudly and confessed
to having coughing fits, a little fluid
lost in my lungs. I choked, but he wasn't
really listening. So I told him to go tell his new girlfriend
about his dosage problems. Go reenact *Casablanca*
and change the sadder-than-thou ending. See if I care.
All of which was my way of saying that I have whispered
to the stars about how he makes them
look bad. Unlike the stars, for example,
he has opened his mouth and said my name.
Does he really think the parting of his lips

is just a soft coincidence? All of which,
unfortunately, is my way of hoping
he will look up and, out of fear,
spill my name as if it were his blood.
Or on the other hand, Mr. No Celestial Comment could
die immediately because his purpose
has been realized: I adore him for no reason.
But, as my ex-boyfriend, he is dead now
in many ways. Or so I tell myself.

3

I was young once, eight or ten, and this
involved a backyard where nobody
watched me. I played a game called 1, 2, 3 . . .
I'm Perfect Starting Now. I would get
so far as to say "I like mystery and
cheese sandwiches" into a wind that messed my hair and then
I would have to start all over again.
OK, starting *now*. Now. Well, then, now. What about now?
But sometimes whole minutes passed in which I did not
let myself or any other nations down.
If I would've known then the kind of battles
I'd actually win, I would've become a nun.
Or so I tell myself. I would've
stopped thinking of my hair as a contribution and grown
at least one perfect English garden rose.
I would've misted the air until a reluctant
bloom opened like a fool's heart to me
and allowed me to say to my occasional group
of hopeless visitors, "Hey! do you think these petals
are a joke? Is it *funny* to you
that they can come so close to falling apart
but never do? You know, you can only find
this color on babies and inside clouds. Usually only wounds

can be this open. How could something
this flawless that grows out of dirt
not have a message? Haven't you felt this
opening inside you all along?"

Grace Lies Down on the Hood of Her Car

God stutters. Indiana is proof.
Corn. Corn. Corn. Corn. Corn. Girl.

I'm a seed, a stalk,
only He said me wrong. I'm a slip

of His tongue. Among the green rows,
I'm unheard of. Watch out, stalk and tassel.

I may end peace on earth
by getting up and walking.

Who am I kidding?
The twenty-ton sky? The token tree?

In a field of corn I'm as brief
as a kiss good-bye.

And I don't want to end this way.
I want to be in someone's mouth

and be repeated until I'm as monotonous
as a hill of daisies.

In Indiana God should have said
"lover" more often instead of trying so hard

to make His four new directions
suddenly meaningless.

Six hours of corn
and me not even a millisecond.

This is when I need a lover.
Together we would add up

to half a second.
He could take me into his mouth

and make me last.
In the face of flatness with no sides,

of bottom, bottom, bottom with no top,
I put up very close walls.

In Indiana I could be like sanity to him
except he could dig his fingers into me.

Billy Pretends to Understand Grace

The house is too silent for me to move.
The bright machine of morning has a jam.
My hand lies missing my cock, and I worry
I'll never cry again. Grace is angry
about the way I look against the sheets
and the way the trees look against the sky.
Then the smell of coffee—the kindest
visitor to come by all week. She must be
making a breakfast that will feed whatever
is weak in us. She must love me again.
Maybe for finally digging up enough dirt
and planting a whole paycheck of lilies.
She must know what it did to my knees. She must know
I'd never filled anything until it was full.

Mostly Mick Jagger

1

Thank god he stuck his tongue out.
When I was twelve I was in danger
of taking my body seriously.
I thought the ache in my nipple was priceless.
I thought I should stay very still
and compare it to a button,
a china saucer,
a flash in a car side-mirror,
so I could name the ache either big or little,
then keep it forever. He blew no one a kiss,
then turned into a maw.

After I saw him, when a wish moved in my pants,
I nurtured it. I stalked around my room
kicking my feet up just like him, making
a big deal of my lips. I was my own big boy.
I wouldn't admit it then,
but he definitely cocks his hip
as if he is his own little girl.

2

People ask me—I make up interviews
while I brush my teeth—"So, what do you remember best
about your childhood?" I say
mostly the drive toward Chicago.
Feeling as if I'm being slowly pressed against the skyline.
Hoping to break a window.
Mostly quick handfuls of boys' skin.
Summer twilights that took forever to get rid of.
Mostly Mick Jagger.

3

How do I explain my hungry stare?
My Friday night spent changing clothes?
My love for travel? I rewind the way he says "now"
with so much roof of the mouth.
I rewind until I get a clear image of myself:
I'm telling the joke he taught me
about my body. My mouth is stretched open
so I don't laugh. My hands are pretending
to have just discovered my own face.
My name is written out in metal studs
across my little pink jumper.
I've got a mirror and a good idea
of the way I want my face to look.
When I glance sideways my smile should twitch
as if a funny picture of me is taped up
inside the corner of my eye.
A picture where my hair is combed over each shoulder,
my breasts are well-supported, and my teeth barely show.
A picture where I'm trying hard to say "beautiful."

He always says, "This is my skinny rib cage,
my one, two chest hairs."
That's all he ever says.
Think of a bird with no feathers
or think of a hundred lips bruising every inch of his skin.
There are no pictures of him hoping
he said the right thing.

Doll Up

I dream of a Ledaean body, bent
Above a sinking fire . . .
—W.B. Yeats, "Among School Children"

I need to go doll up.
I need to run and get the crown jewels,
pluck the life out of my eyebrows.
Perfect arcs.
Pinches of rubies.
I believe the fingers of young virgins
left these priceless red marks all over me.
Oh, and parts of me can fly
when I widen my eyes.
Actually the flying is real;
it's my long, veinless legs
that take work.
Everyone will think of sparrows and guillotines.
Everyone will cry a bit inside.

Fling Beauty.
Let it fall from you in clots.
Get a good sound out of it
when you hit the plate.
Whipped cream isn't just a sex toy;
the *thwack* it makes against the pie
is a teaching technique
for how to say, "I'm leaning in the doorway now."
The princess and the peritoneum.
Everyone knows exquisite women scratch
and drool in their sleep.
Everyone has bent over
a decaying log and felt cocoons twitch
between the disks in their spine.

Let's go make loud tragic joy
behind a bush,

beside an old-fashioned streetlight,
near an exclusive hotel
while we die.
Everything in my life led up
to my inappropriate laughter.
Let's not call our fate tragic joy anymore.
Let's call it that sucking sound we all like so much.
I need a ten-thousand-dollar dress.
I need a pair of scissors.
Cut the indigo fabric off at my realistic waist,
find me the perfect thigh-highs.
We are going out tonight.

Grace Lies in the Backseat
While Her Boyfriend Drives the Backroads
of Southwestern Florida

The number one means nothing
when you're standing next to a banyan tree.
There must be a trick, a cross between CPR and algebra,
I can use to find the original trunk.

The roots don't need the ground, just each other.
The branches have no respect, no desire
to reach up to support the sky.
Down, between, through, alongside, around, within,

they would twist into a wooden fist if they could plan it.
The branches link to look like
young men and their muscles. The leaves clack
to sound like young girls and their tongues.

All afternoon I have been calling
the first part of the tree.
I use important titles:
main snake, national metaphor,

state throat,
middle finger of the forest,
sculpture of the history of birth.
Tree of three hours in the wrong direction.

Tree of never loving one man
but loving the way pants reveal each man's ankle.
Tree of wishbones, of irreconcilable differences:
one-half eyelid,

one-half solar eclipse.
One-half image—uncut emerald,
one-half unrelated word—murderous.
Another shoot is falling as I speak.

Billy's Vision of Grace

She lands next to me. She hides in my heart
and pecks. She's a sudden bird, my own
small, ruffled piece of nowhere. She can't stay.
Her heartbeat forbids it. She leaves me behind,
as blue as a robin's egg in the grass.
She's the color of sand by day, the color
of the bottom of a well at night.
She's the color of everything at night.
She's a charming shape, and so the moon tries
to use her as a stencil. She's what it wants
more and more of. She emerges and emerges.
She's born and born. Not very many things,
maybe only a bird at night, can keep
flying and still seem completely empty.

Pretty

First, come home. Take off your coat and tie.
Now, decide how you feel about wearing yellow satin.
Some enticements: the glare off the fabric
can make skin appear greenish, otherwordly;
yellow satin is often worn tight;
you'll feel slippery.
But since we don't have any light-shaming satin,
put on my black A-line. No, my slip dress. My shift.
Touch the material with your middle finger.

What do you want to say?
These are words you may perform in falsetto:
why, I, you, swish, good-bye.
These are words you may growl in a voice
as low as it can go and still be
controlled by muscles:
yeah, down, hole, thank you, hey, my.
These are lists off the top of my head,
but they're 100 percent accurate.
Practice ambiguous words—
once with your hip cocked and once
with your hair in your face.
See which way works best.

Think of all the mirrored surfaces in the house
and how you've appeared distorted in them.
Include spoons. Feel multiplied.
Now are you getting to know me?
The idea of yourself, scattered and flashing
in all of the drawers and upstairs rooms,
is supposed to feel nice.

The clothes are uncomfortable, conspicuous, right?
The bra too lacy. The hose too tight.
No? You're secure enough?

But imagine that you're not secure enough,
that the nip of new clothing into your skin
confuses important memories you have
of your parents holding you.
Now, when a bride and groom walk by,
you aren't satisfied with only looking
at their shiny hair, their tapered fingers,
their sibilant legs, their exchange of tears.
As soon as you see them, you've gone too far.
You covet the backs of their throats,
the way their stomach muscles crest and stream.
All their unfamiliar buttons.
You forget to envy only one of them.

All this forgetting disturbs you.
Suddenly you're tracing
the definition of the man's muscles
and the lines all point down.
You keep ending up at his feet.
The woman lies down
and her nipples point up at the stars.
When you lean over her
and block the stars, one of your eyes
begins to burn and give off light.
You want to kick people over
so much your calves hurt.
You stand with your legs two feet apart
and wait for the song to start.
You look scared. You look pretty.
So do I, when you finally decide you're ready
to turn around and look at me.

Fifteen Minutes after the Movie

Tick, tick, ticking light and shade
across the batteries, the *Penthouses*,
and the aspirin packages behind the cash register,
the ceiling fan at the Shell station is foreshadowing.
If I lean against a wall,
I will have a destiny. If I lean and exhale smoke,
my destiny will have higher cheekbones, better boots.
The gleam of a ring, a tooth, a chain.
The obscurity of an alley, a face, a pocket.
My life will fall at the feet of whatever
I see first. The movie was no good,
but it was not ashamed. One scene offered confetti
to confuse with the gunfire. There were main characters,
pores I was forced to see up close.
Listen to the clack of my heels,
the sand I grind into the sidewalk, the rhythm
I set up between the newspapers and the gas pump.
The dollar bill sticking out of my wallet
implies a bad decision. I look up
as if on cue and half expect
an old friend to be breathing hard in front of me,
to be carrying a suitcase.
I'm visibly blasé about my keys,
about putting them in the ignition.
The song on the stereo matters
since I'm going to sing it.
"I turned twenty-one in prison doing life without parole."
Who will smash my front end?
Who will run out in front of me?
My decision to drive by the river alone
is worth noting. Each turn of my head
seems choreographed, agonized over
by someone else. I don't appear to know it,
but my life's about to change. Never mind
that I'm badly dressed. Exaggerating

my personality is my only job.
Since I'm green-eyed and short—
scrappy but breakable—
I should be quick to look hurt,
to say "fuck" unexpectedly, the ideal project
for a giving, soft-spoken, divorced,
older man. From between the trees,
he'll wave me down with a flashlight.
A small cut will bleed
over his stupefied eye. I'll be drawn toward the wound,
turn skeptical, stiffen,
not realize I'm going to be happy for the rest of my life.
To my right, a dirt road leads down
to the river. To my right,
a dirt road disappears behind me.
A figure should have staggered out of the woods.
The timing would have been perfect.

Blow Your House Down

So the question becomes—no offense—
are men wolves or are men slop?
Because my heart is definitely a pig.

Each boy sings like a half-wit alone in a barn:
"Little pig heart, little pig heart,
let me in." Oh yes, those farm boys

let loose to form cities
have a way with words. My whiskered heart
breathes—it grunts

through what looks like two
rudimentary bullet holes. Its singing
won't win me any awards:

"Yeah, yeah. Or you'll blow my fucking curlicue
tail off. Well, it's all the same to me."
Same little billy club,

same little manifest destiny
in their pants. So now my girlfriends,
the ones who think anger is like mud—

a bore and the enemy of nice
carpeting—now they sing too.
They sing like Ma and Pa

when the crops die.
They sing loudly, without much hope
and with no trace of syncopation: "What on earth,

if that's what you're calling it
these days, did those boys do to you
to make you hate them,

each and every one of them,
especially the handsome ones
and the ones with smiles

like ice-cream-truck drivers?"
They should know better
than to ask another girl how she feels

about the horse that falls asleep
whenever she tries to ride it.
"Not by a sharp black hair plucked out

of my chinny chin chin." By way of explanation
I get close enough to their faces
that they can smell the just-swallowed

corn on my breath. I make them slightly
dislike me, and I say,
"Hate them?!

Can a jiggle-thighed heart
hate the slop that makes her fat? Can a
succulence hate the teeth that open her?"

Well. They look away then.
They push back the chairs, roll up
the car windows, pull the hats over their ears.

Like it's time to go. Like some great mystery
that always bothered them
finally makes sense.

Grace Lies on the Public Beach

OK, I give in—I am the sea.
I am like the sea.
I make a Great Lake seem small.

I turn it into a testimony to my womb,
to everything I would like to put inside my womb
and would like to feel rise out of me.

I feel everything rise out of me—
love of lotion, invention of skin,
fragrance of fruit, strokes of brilliance.

The tropical islands are tearing me apart.
It's a good pain, the birth of color. But look at me,
I cling so tightly to my bones that I must be

rising out of the woman behind me.
Her mouth is wide-open. The girth of the shore
and my bare shoulders are ripping her apart.

Propped on her elbows, she smiles
and throws her head back, her heels digging
up the beach. The lake wiggles

on a blanket of sand
beside us both. Something in me
is beaming and answering the sun.

The burning heart of things?
No, the man behind me—the man behind
the woman behind me. His white skin,

his pallor's answer is passing through me, calling
to the sun. The sun is saying "yes," the man is saying
"who ya tellin'." He is fresh from his son's mouth.

His son drips the love of his mother.
Her love for him soothes a small spot of skin
near my eye. We're all about to give birth

to crazy, dancing shadows.
We're about to leave this world behind.
The hot sand has plans for us.

Behind me, the young boy shakes
himself off. He has been inside the earth's mouth
and has come out feeling sucked on. He leaves all of us

wearing sequins made of water.
Dazzled, he announces that this is it,
the day without clouds.

He's right, and to celebrate, we all begin to break
into less obvious,
insidious pieces. There are still

parts of us left,
but they are grains so small they're colorless
when they're lifted from the lake floor.

Billy Watches from the Garden

She stands, leans, sits in a hundred positions,
all beautiful. She commands space the way
unexpected daisies take over a table
cluttered with Sunday. She's always dwelled
on the stems, on the thin, on the crisp,
on the few drops of juice there. Her new trick
is forming a whole, feeling the yellow center
her arms and legs hang from, heavy and white.
She loves me and she loves me not. She almost
doesn't need me at all. But I'm always here
to confuse fallen rose petals with
what she might say and to be unable
to pick her. Her own hand behind her head
is perfect, resting learned from a lily.

Invitation for a Dead Friend

Your cousin sounded exactly like you
when she called. She said something to the effect of
"I'm really not Beth. Beth's dead. She committed suicide."
I must have drained her reserves with my giggling.
I don't remember screaming, I remember running
from the place in the hall where my insides
turned to noise. I sat down at my desk
with my face. My little sister had to put her head down
on my bed when she saw it. My nephew
used the back door and ran to the woods.
My dad reached toward me
and fell from a stepladder. I pulled myself
up to my desk and forgot you.
I had to describe my scream. *My body is in the way
of the world becoming a great wind.
All the babies inside me have been torn out,
boneless and surprised.* The surface of my desk
was pure white. It seemed a place I could go to.
I mourned you for less than a minute.
My mom grabbed me and tried to put my face
back inside her.

Remember when you took up space
and could lie next to me? In Saint Paul, lying between
pictures of yourself, lying beside the lights
from the stereo, you turned your head
so no one could see you.
You made your boyfriend's mouth
turn into my mouth, my mouth just like his,
covering your mouth.
We never did get in trouble for that one.
I think we wanted to,
but my hand under your shirt was so quiet.

Boys are still better than being able to get sunshine
inside you, by the way. Each of them carries
a single curled leaf inside his head. I can hear them
opening the future against the back of their teeth.
And the girls get cockier every day. The end of the world,
they've decided, tastes like them.
This isn't about what you are missing.
No matter what I say, it's all two eyes
and a nose. You always wanted to know whether or not
I was going to kiss you again, whether or not everyone was.
We all did. Next to our remarkable, guilty pleasure,
you didn't stand a chance.
I wrote a novel about it, choreographed a ballet:
I said, "You looking straight at me is like, is like, is like."

But look at you now,
when you stand in front of me
all full of lit windows. When you laugh
you sound like a car going by.
Really, look at you. What are you going to do
with all those puddles?
With all those cold, black branches?
The bay stares up like a broken pupil.
What are you going to do with it?

Let's lay you down under its lid.
You can tell me what birds you see
and how the ice you watch through breaks their bodies apart
into only wings, wings. Let the lake
try to cry you, try to move you, try to get you out.
Let the ore boats slowly bless you.
Let's use the ice to keep your face for me.

Glimmer

Middle of February, middle of my forearm.
Sickly white. The skin all over my body
gleams like an eyelid—thin, veiny, waxen.

I should, trees should, something other
than expensive oranges should,
command attention.

I was born with the water that protects my eye
frozen on my lashes. Sickly white.
Now that I'm grown up, I could run naked past snowbanks

and disappear, briefly lose
the definition of my teeth and my heavy breasts.
Heads would turn, send steam up into the air,

and no one would ever know why. The temptation
always drifts in—doorways are a mixed blessing in the cold.
Winter piles up,

and I can either grow longer and drip
like an icicle
or wear a lot of red.

I watch myself appear outside.
Mittens and zippers keep track of me.
When the temperature is below zero, I feel disciplined

just for breathing. The workings of my body
are too distinct for me to care what I look like.
My nose hairs creak when I inhale. My bronchioles

snap into crystals. When I look up,
my lungs begin to twinkle and expand. I have a glimmer
in the corner of my mouth.

In the end, I'm too suggestible. With the sky
pressing against my ribs, I can't stay small enough
for blood to reach my fingertips.

I give up. The snow builds a skin of ice
and crackles while I wait. I don't turn blue. I smile,
breathe in the cold and give up again.

When She Gets Home from the Grocery Store and Notices the Fireflies, Grace Lies Down next to the Driveway

The stars are loose between the houses.
The street of white, unchipped porches
would have me believe we do
get our sprinkling of outer space,
if we stay quiet long enough.

This is the overconfidence bred
by venetian blinds and by painted hooks
from which lobelia baskets are hung
every summer. This is the overconfidence
that gets me out of bed in the morning.

Burn by the back steps. Burn out by the car tire.
Never has apocalypse been as bright blue
or as easy to love and to tease.
My thoughts of rubble never last long.
The doors across the street

always stand. I wish I could doubt
the end of the world will be porch-lit,
a series of sparkles over my neighbor's pool.
The flashes of light reassure me.
The dark reassures me. The lesson of the firefly:

I can expect my smile to be temporary,
my will to be wing-sized.
But the overall effect is beautiful.
The lesson of the firefly:
the delight of large numbers, of losing

track of myself in a long string of zeros.
On 14th Street, the repetition of acorns

and mailboxes is a radical observation.
I can shut up. Life will still stutter.
My revolutionary wish

is for a fresh glass of ice cubes,
a full, chilly hand. All night I'll envy
the fireflies' ability to scatter.
They're lit and they linger
three feet above everyone's yard.

I would show up only at night. I would get less done.
I would see myself repeated
between all the marigolds. Tonight, an aerial view of the town
after everyone has turned on their floodlights
is the only way to describe my mood.

If Billy Were Invisible, Part II

I do have a daydream I feel good about.
Unseen, I touch her in ways I never
would if she could see my bunched face, pulling
eyes, nose, and mouth together even tighter,
as if they were swirling down a drain, as if
that were the best thing that could happen
so I wouldn't see, smell, and taste her,
as if love were a cause for concern, as if
I were trying to stick a needle in her
and didn't want her to feel it but knew
exactly how sharply she would. So in my dream
she feels me but sees only the ceiling
and knows only that beyond the roof
is the blank face of the sun which she lies below
feeling ecstatic for no reason she can name.

Singing the Accident

She'd never loved herself as much, though what was left
of her body made no sense. She was maybe
a thick mix of paints

that had confused itself with a woman.
That had happened before.
Under the special lighting of museums. The cracks

in the windshield took the sun away
in a million rivers, so she was under
special lighting. She was getting brighter

instead of fading. Maybe this whole time
the wrinkles, the expressions she constantly
rearranged on her face were her way of proving

she was an actual person, fully capable
of aching, even without anything actually being wrong.
In the front seat she had very little

structure, and yet she wasn't just a painting. She rang
in the air, like something dear that had been struck.
The wind passed through trees that must have

contained enough silver to make them
instruments. She was one of the sounds
that was made and held without breathing. She was unfinished

but performed anyway, dedicated to
the girlish birch trees that could only watch,
could actually only seem to watch. She was an aria

about seeming, and she was growing quiet.
The trees pulsed discreetly with their fluid
and, against the dash at any rate,

she was like their sap,
or rather she was like a tree that didn't want
to stand up anymore. Which is common enough. The ripples

on rivers and lakes have to come from somewhere.
She was like water torn by a rock or sudden current.
Nothing about her was ugly.

Her body had been one way of doing things,
a convenient way to watch a sleeping baby.
Now she was closer to the baby's sleep, that was all, and closer

to its waking. She was the gurgle in its slippery mouth.
So when she found herself pinned
against the steering wheel, she knew she had finally

begun to sing. Her body was singing of new shapes
it was capable of taking. Her ears hurt
because the song was true invention. The score

could not be written down. The notes may,
she thought, have been birds that had flown away.
Or she could have just been singing insights

she hadn't yet made.
It didn't matter either way. Outside the car,
her audience turned red and hoped for her attention. They swirled

and tried to dance like her burns, tried to be skinless
in their heavy coats, quick to bubble up
in their flawless lives. Her hair conducted them

through the falling background of the leaves
to spell out her name with their faces, to act out her body
and its ruptures with their eyes. How many wanted

to marry her, wanted the chance to slap her face and be unable
to break her glutted heart. She'd never loved herself as much.
She listened to her blood beating time

in everyone else's veins, against the glass, on their hands.
She listened to it sing, louder and louder,
that nothing had ever hurt her.

An Angel Finally Admits What She Knows
to Lou Binkler of Bethany, Missouri

Some people weren't meant to eat a New York strip.
Some people weren't meant to actually touch
the amniotic ocean. Some people, Lou,

weren't meant to wiggle their ten toes
in the sand and say, "Hey!
Those waves are nibbling everything away

besides me!" Some people weren't ever meant
to fall from the sky. Some people,
ya gotta have faith there's a reason for them. They don't even try

to defy gravity, no matter how see-through
my dress or how long
I float, blond and stiff-nippled, right over them.

So I whisper, "I'm not the moon, you fool."
But some people just weren't meant
to understand English. Or time and space.

Some people weren't meant to know the rush of stars
past their terribly bone-encased heads.
But never mind heaven.

Let's start from the beginning.
Some people weren't meant to be born
with two legs. Some people weren't meant to go to college

and then keep a clean house. Some people
weren't meant to perfect their vibrato in a spotlight or even to shake
when they kill a fourteen-point buck. Some people

weren't meant to be let outside. Ever. Some people,
it sounds silly, weren't meant to own pets.
Some people weren't meant to be touched

or inhaled or lifted off the ground.
Or penetrated. Or believed. Or fed.
Or lived with. Some people

weren't meant to sleep well or to put up
with this world past age twenty-five. Some people
weren't meant to see their own blood. Or to give any away.

To save any rare babies. Do you see the golden plan, Lou?
Some people weren't meant to shoot a pop can
off a fence post and feel good about it.

Some people weren't meant to look at the sun
and blink as slowly as other people pull
a blanket over a sleeping baby. Some people

weren't meant to be alone. They weren't meant
to ever stop smiling, sleeping, and holding
the sticky baby fingers

that pull their mouths down
into a terrible drool. Some people
weren't meant to stop kissing long enough to thank god.

Some people, let me try to touch you
where you've never been touched before while I say this.
Some people, I'm sorry, Lou, my touch must feel

like your own familiar ache plus a little warm air.
Some people—lift your damp face to me, Lou—
weren't meant to ever fall in love in the first place.

The Return to Skin

What do you get when you cross a cheekbone
and a pistol grip? Besides a hairline fracture.
You get ideas, inaccurate ones
like "no problem," "the son of a bitch
will pay for this," and "my soul is rich,"
and "the scary part's over."

You get a ghost. Not necessarily
of the dead variety, but definitely
of the incorporeal variety.
The faceless type. The thin-air kind of girl.
Shhhhhh. I've become
the girl no one can ever hurry
into the men's bathroom with a gun.
I was on the verge—surely—
of impressing a man
with the possibilities of my limbs,
then I lost my body in a terrible accident.
Soon I got tired of hovering
in the loveless air, so I rested
under men's chins and in the declivities
where their muscles attach to bone.
The men often mistook me for their own breath,
and on a wild night, so did I.

I had a good thing going once with a smile and an inner thigh.
I had many rooms in my mansion.
Then I had to learn to cross and uncross my legs,
without legs. With no gut,
I had to rephrase hunger and desire as questions:
Is the pistol loaded?
Is the pistol grip ivory?
At parties I say,
I have decided against elbows and company.
In tense moments I well up in other people's eyes.

I like to ease myself back into reality sometimes,
on a patio filled with people, snapdragons,
glass tables, and ice cubes.
The reality is that people drape their arms
over the chairs next to them. They smile at the view.
They bring the world inside them through the tiniest holes,
and there's always more of the world left.
People love having tendons,
love reaching for sips, pointing at sailboats, and squeezing knees.
I'm going to whisper to one of them soon:

Haver, Reacher, Pointer, Squeezer, call me back to you
one finger at a time. Leave an impression
on the sofa that you can show me and then say,
"Now you try." What do you get
when you cross a sunset
and a ghost? Besides longing.
You get the desire to start over.
Shoulder-Tracer, Hair-Braider, Face-Noticer,
draw me in the air,
one bone for each hour
until you can hold me.

We Are Gathered Here Today

Wouldn't it be a good idea if
we got married? I take thee salty, sweet,
and tart to be my lawful wedded flavors.
I take thee hornet, squirrel, and sandpiper
to be my skittish, hungry brides in sickness
and in health. Our life together will come

and go like daisies, and when winter comes
we'll have our babies: ice, pine, and moon if
we survive the stiff, blue morning sickness.
So I take thee chill and cramp that sweeten
my stringy muscles. I'll pay the piper
for the song of fever, the chef for each flavor

of my slow burn. I take thee sweat that flavors
my kisses and the ones who kiss me. How come
twining stars in my veil is only a pipe dream?
I've taken them for richer and for poorer, and if
nothing else they often lie beside me, sweetly
dying of time, which is my favorite sickness.

I agree with the little girls who are lovesick:
the hungry never get to taste the best flavors.
Good thing lying in bed alone leaves the sweetest
sting of honey on the tongue. When real life comes,
bringing midnight, white nightgowns, and grown-up skin, if
it can, I hope it wakes us. We're unsmoked pipes

until then. We're everything else too. I pipe
the endlessness into the ocean. I take its seasickness
to have, hold, and die from. Especially if
while I drown it savors me like a new flavor.
In the end, which is my favorite time, it all comes
down to need, which is what I can give you, my sweet

husband, wife, betrayer, mistress. My sweet
coo, fall, wing. My silk, velvet, satin piping.
I take thee full, weak, perfumed, wilting. Please come
home, which is like a box. Love is a sickness
I hate to cure. Time, scent, dirt, flavor,
we'd make promises if only we could.

Notes

Several poems here quote lyrics from songs, and I would like to thank those artists.

"Cranberry Juice" quotes lyrics from "To Live Is to Fly" by Townes Van Zandt.

"My Mom's Cobalt-Blue Glass Collection" quotes lyrics from "Like I Used to Do" by Tim O'Brien.

"The E-String Strut (or Heaven According to the E String on Steve Earle's Acoustic Guitar)" quotes lyrics from "Hurtin' Me, Hurtin' You" and "Guitar Town" by Steve Earle.

"Fifteen Minutes after the Movie" quotes lyrics from "Mama Tried" by Merle Haggard.

CATIE ROSEMURGY currently teaches at Northwest Missouri State University and is a co-editor of the *Laurel Review*. Her poems have appeared in the *Best American Poetry 1997, Poetry Northwest, Michigan Quarterly Review,* and *Ploughshares,* among other magazines and anthologies. She splits her time between Maryville, Missouri, and Escanaba, Michigan.

The text of *My Favorite Apocalypse* was set in Adobe Caslon, a face drawn by Carol Twombly in 1989, and based on the work of William Caslon (c. 1692–1766), an English engraver, punchcutter, and typefounder.

This book was design by Wendy Holdman, set in type by Stanton Publication Services, Inc., and manufactured by Bang Printing on acid-free paper.

Graywolf Press is a not-for-profit, independent press. The books we publish include poetry, literary fiction, and cultural criticism. We are less interested in best-sellers than in talented writers who display a freshness of voice coupled with a distinct vision. We believe these are the very qualities essential to shape a vital and diverse culture.

Thankfully, many of our readers feel the same way. They have shown this through their desire to buy books by Graywolf writers; they have told us this themselves through their e-mail notes and at author events; and they have reinforced their commitment by contributing financial support, in small amounts and in large amounts, and joining the "Friends of Graywolf."

If you enjoyed this book and wish to learn more about Graywolf Press, we invite you to ask your bookseller or librarian about further Graywolf titles; or to contact us for a free catalog; or to visit our award-winning web site that features information about our forthcoming books.

We would also like to invite you to consider joining the hundreds of individuals who are already "Friends of Graywolf" by contributing to our membership program. Individual donations of any size are significant to us: they tell us that you believe that the kind of publishing we do *matters*. Our web site gives you many more details about the benefits you will enjoy as a "Friend of Graywolf"; but if you do not have online access, we urge you to contact us for a copy of our membership brochure.

www.graywolfpress.org

Graywolf Press
2402 University Avenue, Suite 203
Saint Paul, MN 55114
Phone: (651) 641-0077
Fax: (651) 641-0036
E-mail: wolves@graywolfpress.org

Graywolf Press is dedicated to the creation and promotion of thoughtful and imaginative contemporary literature essential to a vital and diverse culture. For further information, visit us online at:

www.graywolfpress.org.

Other Graywolf titles you might enjoy are:

Among Women by Jason Shinder
As for Dream by Saskia Hamilton
Domestic Work by Natasha Trethewey
Some Ether by Nick Flynn
Bewitched Playground by David Rivard
Donkey Gospel by Tony Hoagland